Hanging
Ghosts

Hanging Ghosts

Poems by Sheldon Flett

HANGING GHOSTS
Poems by Sheldon Flett

Copyright © Sheldon Flett, 2023

Thanks to PENCIL PHOTO SKETCH APP.
For the transformation of my pictures

Published by Sheldon Flett, Barrhead, Canada

ISBN:
    Paperback   978-1-77354-472-4
        ebook   978-1-77354-473-1

Publication assistance by

PAGEMASTER
PUBLISHING
PageMaster.ca

Dedication

I would like to dedicate this book of poems to
my lovely wife Barbara Flett, who inspired me
to bring out my inner thoughts and ideas.

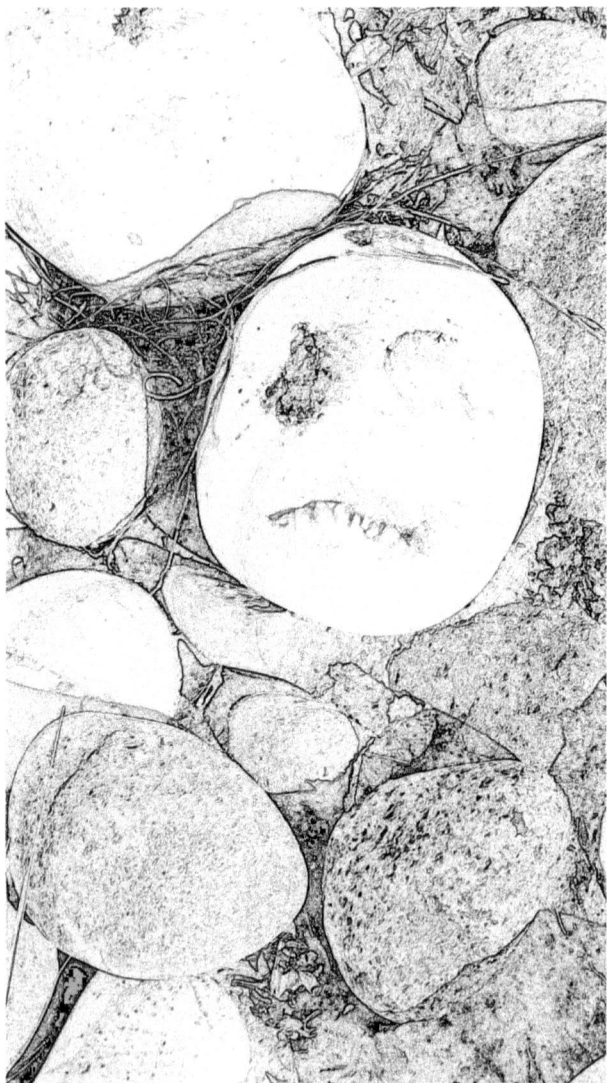

Hanging Ghosts

Life goes on no matter what, you might be smart you might be rich you might just have it all, king of that hill. You look around at all the working people feeling down while you fill your pockets all day long, but some of us ghosts have no fear, as you laugh and grin all day and all night, just in spite. And one day it'll all make sense, as you trip in your soul you'll feel temptation start to grow, a twisting rope, hoping no one will ever know, you'll slip as the money starts to flow. Just when you think you have it all, someone frowning comes along, sees that you're no longer a king on that hill, shouting, yelling, "Bring it all!" Because that one little person found your flaw, now all over town everyone is looking down, for when ghosts hang around, eventually the gallows will be found.

More than just a Gun

Shooting cans and being cool, crack barrel slip one in,
squeeze that trigger smell that smoke, watch as the Coke
cans disappear, remembering grandpa passing it down, you
learned how to shoot before you could crawl. More than just
a gun, shooting bottles in the dark just so you can see the
spark, impressing girls out by the lake, betting your buddies
the glass will break. More than just a gun, with every shot
you feel him there, steady hands have no fear, squeeze that
trigger, raise that beer. More than just a gun, as the years
go by, you're that man standing there, gun in hand, a little
shake, left to right, target on, in the sights you let it go, but
not in spite, to pass it down to the next in line.

Mirror

Mirror in the corner standing tall, taking reflections all day long. People turn to you and speak, others dance or take a peek, some cry or silently weep, you watch them as they shave, or brush their teeth. In Germany you were born, metallic silver glass to cap, a gold frame to fill the gap. You watch as we grow from a child with first step to an adult, oh how we crept. As people we were scared to break, for seven years we would not sleep. I respect all those years you watched over me as I grew. Looking back now I am old, reflecting on days gone by, hoping I will never say goodbye. In a box you will go, to watch the next one as they grow. Never crack or take a break, you will always be there for us to have a look.

Monster

Lying in my bed, I review the things in my head. Some
are bad, some are sad, some are exciting, some are mad,
but there are some evil ones around the bend. Jumping up,
have a look, nothing's there but a ticking clock! As the dark
creeps in the room, nothing's there, an empty tomb. Playing
dead, a chill in my bones, realizing I'm there all alone,
pulling my blankets up tight, there's something there in
the night. I thought it was a ticking clock, but it's really my
beating heart!
Things get louder in my head as I try to put them to bed.
Hoping the light will be coming soon, I scan that empty
room. Nothing there but flowing tears, before the alarm's
about to speak, thoughts in my head I try to shake, now I
know there's a monster when awake.

Night

As you walk in the night there's nothing there, just an
empty sight but for the moon glowing bright. You can smell
the emptiness of the night, a chill runs through your bones
as it steals your light. You try to keep your wits as the night
steals your breath, you can't move or make a sound, there's
something in the dead of night, your breath you see forever
white. As something squeezes your lungs so tight, as you
think your last breath leaves, there's an angel by your side!
Something grabs you from behind, you turn around, dark as
night, there's nothing there in your sight. A beam from up
above, a glimpse of day, as you look past the light, all is good
with the night.

As I Walk through Time

As I walk through time, I reflect on days gone by. I keep in mind all the good times, turn my cheek to the bad. I realize in life you are dealt a hand, what to do with it is totally up to you. I had a straight, then three of a kind, then I had four queens and thought I was the king!

Turned out I was being played, the joker at whom everyone could laugh. But who's laughing now? I've got a royal flush! Best hand out there! And I promise until the day I die, I will always protect this hand and live every moment as it goes by, for you only once in a lifetime get a royal hand. So as my time tics by, I will always love my loving wife. Forever yours, a joker who met his queen of hearts.

Light Flickers

The light flickers in the night, an old wood stove is
burning bright, and echoes in the dark send ghostly shivers
through the night. As the wind whistles by, the fire makes
unfamiliar cries. It crackles and sparks, there's something
else there with the wind, a soft sound settles in. Like a thief
in the night, you hear it knocking at the door, and then the
scratching on the floor, then the mournful cry. As the cold
comes rushing in it runs up you like the wind! You wish you
had something to hold, you're all alone, you've still got that
flicker of light, you pray on your knees, please don't go out,
as howls from the dark turn to whispers with the sparks,
there is only soot and ash to stir, no more light to flicker
bright.

Shadow

During the night it's never found, but is in the corners and hallways bound, or in the attic with a light, crazy dreams fill the night, like someone standing still, it's always there to fill the room, until you turn off the light, it disappears with the night. Where it goes we'll never know, but by your side you feel it there, black as night, there is no glow to see the dark, you can't see it there. By the light it will be found, for light really is the foe, at least by day you can see it there, standing tall, looking down, just a shadow in the room.

Leaves

When the leaves begin to fall, there are echos down the
hall, things turning in the wind with unfamiliar spins,
and ghostly figures come to play. Your heart pounds in the
dark, you smell the air, feel the despair, all around it smells
like death, a chill begins to creep, there's no more red in
your cheeks, nothing there but the beat of a heart you can't
cheat! The shadows begin to speak, you have no feeling in
your feet as you watch the leaves blow by and another tear
begins to dry. The blood starts to flow, racing fast with every
cry, another leaf begins to dance in a whirlwind of chance.
Images in your head, orange, yellow, especially red that fall
to the ground, looking dead, as a feeling comes back to play
in a night so cold and dark nothing there but a lonely heart.
Now the night begins to speak, it's time to go, whisper the
trees, there is nothing left but leaves to crunch beneath
your feet, the wind howls, leaves blow, floating fluttering
all around, now you're home looking down, leaves blowing
on the ground, the door begins to slam, you run so fast you
can't feel the ground, as the trees shed all, no leaves are left
to brighten the night.

Feather Pen

As you dip your feather in, the ink begins to play, images
dancing in your head, the paper shudders, as the ink starts
to sink, the paper getting darker, black, blacker on the page,
as the feather dances away, soon there is no white left, more
paper starts to glide across the table, soon the ink begins to
dwindle, the end is getting near, the lantern starts to dim,
an old song you start to hum, the dark comes ripping down,
now it's empty, no more light, no writing on the papers
white, there's not a drop of ink, it was all in your head, no
dripping quill on your lap, there's no going back, no feather
pen to end the spell, it's all done, just an empty room.

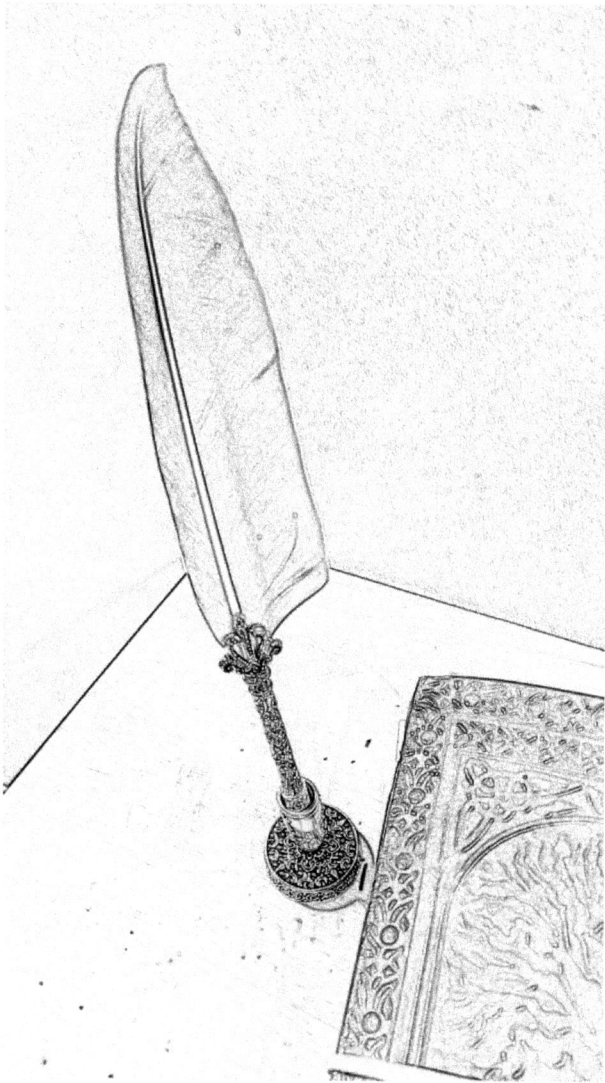

Fools Kissing Fools

Sitting on bar stools, tying to be cool, breaking all the rules, playing the game, trying not to lose. Roll that dice, feel the night, hoping it never ends. Fools kissing fools. Shoot some shots, drink that beer. Lights are flashing, beer we're stacking, no last call in sight. Fools kissing fools. Playing pool, crack that rack, chalk that cue, stripes or solids, what will sink? Win that game, playing doubles, playing to win. Drop that eight ball, begin again. Fools kissing fools. As the night gets deeper the drinks get steeper, fill our glasses cheers to win. Things get cloudy, start to spin, pretty soon the balls aren't going in, last call is all you hear, as you're whispering in her ear. Fools kissing fools. The night turns into day, as you try to find your keys. Where am I what did I do, nothing looks familiar in the room. Empty bed no one around, your heart starts to pound, as it sinks to the floor, everything is gone, but a note on the bathroom mirror. Fools kissing fools.

House

This old house, there is a glow. With the night you can
feel the flow of life, in every corner there's dust and mites,
but that's ok you know the way, as we clean in the night,
the house will always be there to fill with light, and speak
through the floors with every step, creaking snapping, in
the walls and down the halls little whispers hit the ground,
an old wood stove crackles, with every log there is a sound,
as each season begins it will be there with every spark,
protecting us and never sleep as the nights begin to speak,
our old house has a beat, with every door and windows
open, there is always someone having spoken of your clutter
and things around, but only us it has to please, for this is
the house we have chosen, with the love and care it has
given, we will be there to cut the ribbon for all the years of
standing tall, it's our house that will never fall.

Buried Deep

You walk forward in life, sometimes looking back, when it comes upon you like a blast in the dark. Some days you don't want to go backwards, but sometimes you can't leave it hanging, like a rope in a shaft, swinging swaying in the wind, hoping these memories will fade away. You try with all your might, but the past wants to be remembered instead of put away. The good times will always be there, but a darkness is waiting, waiting to be set free like a canary in a cage, waiting for that latch to open so it can fly, just wanting to leave, in the back of your mind, buried deep, deep in that mine.

Waiting for that dynamite blast to find new tunnels to uncover, they dig and dig to recover all those bodies you tried to cover, and now they're lying all around the room. You tried to warn them, silly fools!

Memory Loss

We dance around the living room floor, hand in hand, foot on floor. Locking eyes so deep, hoping this night will keep singing songs, whispering winds won't end it all. Never spoken, the love we have is never broken.

We look in each other's eyes, who are you, with a look I've never seen, a person with the bluest eyes I would never forget, even blind, the eyes of my blue-eyed angel looking back. Even though it's hard to find, is this my sock I left behind? I get so mad, is this my life, or am I blind? I can't remember, I can't find, what happened to the friends I left behind, then I see someone I know, happy as I start to go, I look who are you? I start to speak, I am so sorry to my wife, I will always love you, have no doubt, for if I forget, my heart will always pound, and never forget you, for my wife I married and always keep, even if I forget, your words for me always speak, never forgotten in my mind, just a ticking clock in time.

You got Out Bid

You sit and think, what is this worth, is it special or just another thing on a shelf, did I spend too much, is it well worth my bid, you go higher as another bidder starts, bidding against you! Up by 5 then 20, where should I stop, there's nothing against me! I will stop, let it go, I didn't need it anyway, I've got two more on the shelf, maybe it's worth it, I think to myself, one more bid then it's mine!! As the devil turns around and says, you might think you have won, but I just got word you're out of time! Going once going twice, back in line. You just got out bid!

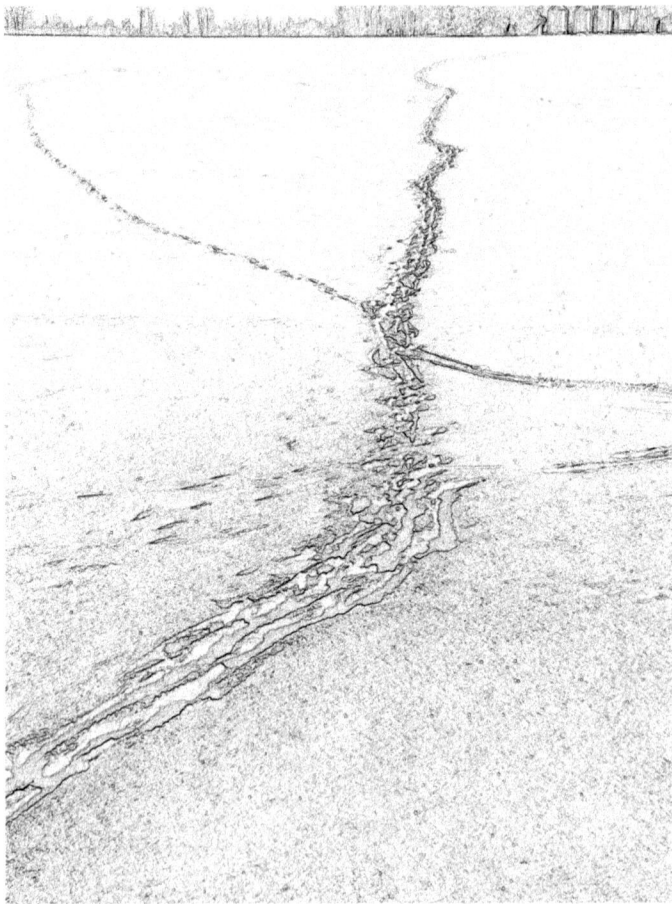

Tracks

Tracks in the snow, where do they go? Through the trees, and around the trunk, down a groundhog hole, up the stump. You wonder what they might be, you follow them for a little bit, as you hug your frosty mitt. Tracks all around, going sideways up and down, how many creatures come out at night? You want to say you know them all, but one stands out above them all, it's not a deer or a moose or cow on the loose. You're lost and all alone, times are tough, you're in a bad way, you think there's no other play. The only tracks you will always know are the ones you follow to get back home.

Train

We move along the tracks, some moving forward some
moving back. Not knowing what's around the bend, straight
stretch, or through the mountains hold on tight because
in the tunnels there is no light, the sound of a train across
the tracks puts you in a little trance, in your head that's
all you hear, broken up with a whistle blow, the sounds of
night rip across the sky, no more poles flying by, no more
counting as your passing by. The night takes you with a
grip that holds so tight, you fight to stay awake, to see the
dark come to play, as your eyelids start to win, you go down
deep, within dreams start to creep, stealing your imagina-
tion wild, as the whistle talks out loud, your heart jumps
with every sound. You made it, destination found! The train
starts slowing down, this doesn't look like what I sought, did
I sleep through my stop and miss it? The steam all around
starts to disappear smoke and all. A fire red sky glowing,
volcanic rocks bubble, something wrong, temperature's
high! Is this the last ride, as you sit inside too scared to
move or go outside, I'm dreaming, you think, I know I never
bought a ticket for this ride. As the man comes round to say
this is your last stop, get off the train, he grabs your arms
as he says, there's no more track, you are out of time, cry
and plead all you want, for this is your place to stay! Please
watch your step as you go, we wouldn't want you to slip and
fall below.

Witches' Hair

Witches' hair witches' hair, down the fox hole up the shrub, silver hair that turns to dust, as the day turns into night, nothing but black is in your sight. Your heart is racing with itself, there's something there that you can see, glowing eyes ripping teeth! Witches' hair witches hair, as you cry for help, not a sound, as the hair stands up on your neck, you whip around to feel the breath. It's just the wind come to rest. Witches' hair witches' hair, you try to run, your legs are numb, as you feel your way, there's nothing ahead but paths of grey. By the glow of moonlight you can see something there, crackling in the silent dead of night, something just doesn't feel right. Witches' hair witches' hair, you've had enough, please end this night, as the claws enter your skin, a familiar chill, something has you, you just can't scream. Her hands are locked around your dreams, as you wake in your bed, you look at your hands, bloody red! Witches' hair witches' hair.

LOVES ♥
BARBIE!

Clown

We used to make children laugh and smile, give them a balloon animal and watch their eyes shine, honk your nose, or fall to the ground, juggle balls all day long.

Something happened long ago, as they've seen our teeth begin to grow, our smiles turn to evil grins, the children lost the flow of loving laughing as we go. Now I sit alone, sad and lonely, nothing left, a horn for a nose I leave to rest, painted face, hair so bright, never ever going to see the light, in a trunk I will go, tucked away, with my heavy heart, no more the clown to steal the part, for there'll be no more clowning around.

Spider's Web

It makes its way through the thickest brush, hanging overhead, without a sound it starts to spin, silky ropes begin to float as the web takes its post. Hours go by, watch as the web outlasts the wind and rain. Looking like a stained glass window, pillars strong and framed to last, a masterpiece, echoes of Notre Dame cathedral. You feel sorry for the bug that took a wrong turn and started to squirm. First mistake was starting to shake, the vibrations start a wave, the spider starts to crave, crawling down he sees his prey on the altar, penitent, no more fight! As he slips up beside, pointed fangs and many eyes, the teeth sink deep inside, numbs his food before he eats, likes it warm, scared and pale. He munches down, the bug now knowing cold and frail, that the spider likes his communion still alive. The bug just can't feel the death inside. The spider spins and wraps, tucks it away for another day, when a vibration starts a dance, oh what's this, stuck in a trance, another prey!

First in Line

'Thank god, first in line' is what everyone thinks standing
in line, a line for us to wait in as the world goes by, what are
we missing standing in line, what's wrong with this person
at the till, wrong pin, or card, is it cash or credit, did they hit
the wrong button, or run out of time?

What's going on, I should've been done and home by now,
feet up and watching the news, of all the things happening
in the world, people rushing around trying to be first in line,
just as you think, it's time to relax, out of milk, and beer, no
wine, run down to the general store, rush in, thank god, first
in line!

Don't Walk Upon the Graves

Flickering shimmering in the dark, one hopes everything will be alright. Ghostly moon hovers overhead because tonight is the night of restless souls. It is all hallows eve, when they say the dark comes out to play, and ghostly figures, shattered dreams, undead hearts come out for prey. You're wishing they'd have stayed deep inside their own graves, the shadows creep as the night drifts on by, an eerie cry hits your bones, like a rock from the sky. Your mind is racing playing tricks, as you're running through the sticks. Every branch grabs your arms, the ground tearing scratching finding harm. As you run there is something wrong, the ground feels like a sponge, you're sinking as they're pulling you down, your nails start to bleed while you're scratching pulling trying to breathe. The ground is falling in around, crushing smashing feel the cold. As your last breath starts to go, you look up to see the glow, it's a tombstone with no name, just a saying, Don't Walk Upon the Graves!

PM Store Author's QR Code
https://pagemasterpublishing.ca/by/sheldon-flett/

To order more copies of this book, find books by other
Canadian authors, or make inquiries about publishing your
own book, contact PageMaster at:

PageMaster Publication Services Inc.
11340-120 Street, Edmonton, AB T5G 0W5
books@pagemaster.ca
780-425-9303

catalogue and e-commerce store
PageMasterPublishing.ca/Shop

Index of Titles

www.ingramcontent.com/pod-product-compliance
Lightning Source LLC
Chambersburg PA
CBHW060540030426
42337CB00021B/4367